HOW WE LIVED...

IN THE SOUTHERN COLONIES

HOW WE LIVED...

IN THE SOUTHERN COLONIES

by Deborah Kent

BENCHMARK BOOKS

MARSHALL CAVENDISH
NEW YORK

ACKNOWLEDGMENT

*For his generous assistance and expert advice, the author wishes to thank
Clarence G. Seckel, Jr., Curriculum Coordinator in the Social Studies,
East Saint Louis School District 189, East Saint Louis, Illinois.*

Benchmark Books
Marshall Cavendish Corporation
99 White Plains Road
Tarrytown, New York 10591-9001

Copyright © 2000 by Deborah Kent

• • •

Library of Congress Cataloging-in-Publication Data
Kent, Deborah
In the southern colonies / Deborah Kent
p. cm—(How we lived)
Includes bibliographical references and index.
Summary: Describes various aspects of the contrasting life styles of the rich and the poor
early settlers in the southern colonies including homes, food, work, religion, education.
ISBN 0-7614-0908-4 (lib.bdg.)
1. Southern States Social life and customs—To 1775—Juvenile literature.   2. Frontier and pioneer life—
Southern States Juvenile literature.   3.Pioneers—Southern States—History—17th century—
Juvenile literature.   [1. Southern States—Social life and customs—to 1775.   2. Frontier and pioneer life—Southern States.
3. Pioneers.]   I. Title.   II. Series.
F212.K46   2000   98-20318   975'.02—dc21   CIP   AC

• • •

Printed in Hong Kong
1 3 5 6 4 2

• • •

BookDesigner: Judith Turziano
Photo Researcher: Debbie Needleman

• • •

PHOTO CREDITS

Front cover: Courtesy of the Colonial Williamsburg Foundation; pages 2–3: The Metropolitan Museum of Art,
New York, Gift of Edgar William and Bernice Chrysler Garbisch (1963. 63.201.3) (Detail); pages 6–7, 8, 14, 16, 22, 32–33:
North Wind Picture Archives; page 10: The Jamestown Yorktown Educational Trust; pages 12–13, 40–41: Corbis/Bettmann;
page 15: National Gallery of Art, Gift of Edgar William and Bernice Chrysler Garbisch (1953.5.89); page 18: John Lewis Stage/
The Image Bank; pages 19, 21, 34, 48, 53, 57: Colonial Williamsburg Foundation; pages 24–25: Abby Aldrich Rockefeller
Folk Art Center, Williamsburg, VA (Detail–*Portrait of Two Children* by Badger); pages 26, 30: Richard Nowitz/Corbis;
page 27: Cralle/The Image Bank; pages 36–37, 42–43, 45, 50–51, 52: Stock Montage; page 54: Scala/Art Resource, NY

Contents

1
The New Discovered Land

"Our men were destroyed by cruel diseases, [such] as swellings, fluxes, [and] burning fevers, and by wars. Some departed suddenly, but for the most part they died of mere famine. There were never Englishmen left in a foreign country in such a misery as we were in this new discovered Virginia."

—GEORGE PERCY, ONE OF VIRGINIA'S
FIRST COLONISTS, 1610

In 1611 George Percy boarded a ship at Jamestown in Virginia, bound for England. He had lived in Virginia for four long years, battling hunger and disease. Now he headed home. As he watched the shore disappear behind him, he must have breathed a sigh of relief.

Much of our information about Jamestown comes from the accounts of George Percy and other Engish colonists. The colonists who founded

Instead of the gold they had expected, the colonists arriving on the Virginia shore found nothing but a wilderness to be tamed.

THE FIRST ENDURING COLONY

The first lasting settlement in the thirteen colonies was James-town, Virginia, founded in 1607. The early colonists at Jamestown spent most of their time searching for gold. They were reluctant to plant crops or build permanent shelters. Winter caught them unprepared, and many died of hunger and cold. The colony seemed doomed until Captain John Smith emerged as its leader. Smith forced the colonists to build houses and work in the fields. He announced that anyone who did not work would not eat. Smith wrote detailed accounts of his life in Virginia. In one, he described being captured by Indians who planned to put him to death. According to Smith, the chief's twelve-year-old daughter Pocahontas persuaded her father to spare his life. The story of John Smith and Pocahontas is an American legend.

Jamestown, Virginia, in 1607 came with high hopes. They were convinced that the New World overflowed with gold and precious gems. These early colonists had little interest in building strong houses or raising crops. They wanted only to search the woods for treasure. Soon their supplies of food ran low. Winter winds howled through their rough wooden shelters. Disease ravaged their ranks. To make matters worse, the colonists had several bloody skirmishes with neighboring Indians. Within months, nearly half of the newcomers died.

Twelve years after its founding, the settlement at Jamestown was still a modest affair. Here, a make-shift marketplace draws the villagers to the town square.

The colonists found no gold in Virginia. Some, like George Percy, returned to England in bitter disappointment. But many others remained. As the years passed, more and more people crossed the Atlantic to join them. New settlements grew up in other parts of Virginia. Eventually a British colony began in the Carolinas to the south. Finally, more than a century after the founding of Jamestown, the British established the colony of Georgia.

Virginia, North and South Carolina, and Georgia were the southernmost of England's thirteen colonies. Life in these southern colonies was very different from colonial life farther north. In the North most people lived on small farms. In the southern colonies, farms tended to be much larger, and they were set farther apart. To work these large farms, or plantations, wealthy colonists used slaves of African descent. Slavery existed throughout the thirteen colonies. But far more slaves lived in the South than anywhere else. Slavery became a part of every aspect of southern life.

Life in the southern colonies is a study in contrasts. The rich lived in luxury. Their slaves owned nothing, not even their own lives. But these extremes do not tell the whole story. The colonies were home to many humble farmers and tradespeople, and to a number of free black people as well. The homes, furnishings, and clothing of the southern colonists offer us a glimpse into what life was like back then.

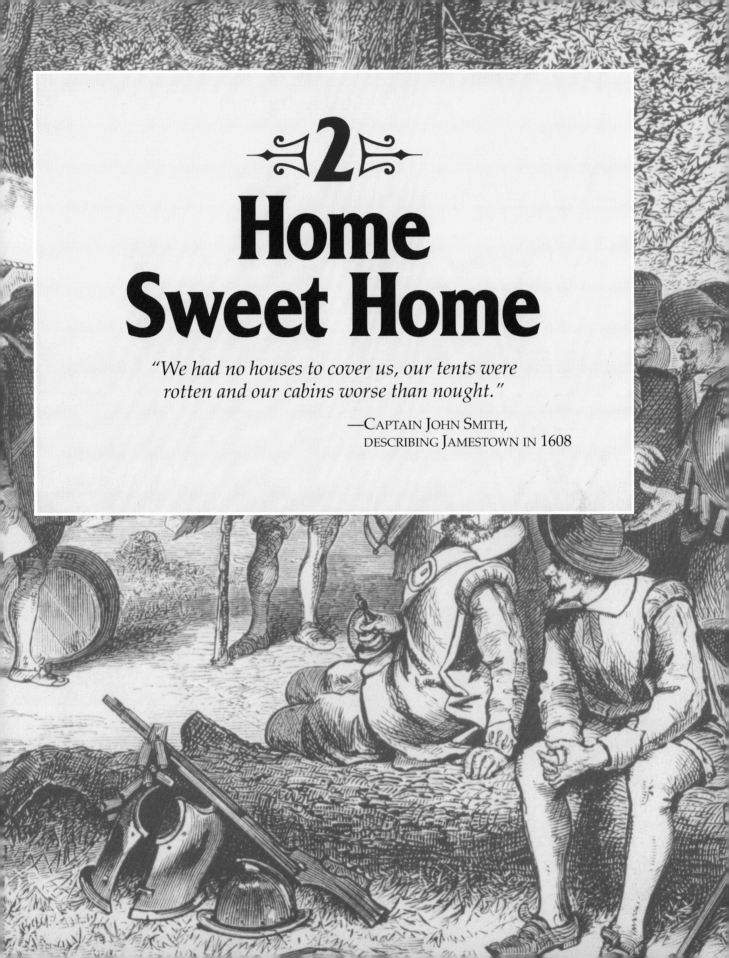

2
Home
Sweet Home

"We had no houses to cover us, our tents were rotten and our cabins worse than nought."

—Captain John Smith,
describing Jamestown in 1608

THE GREAT HOUSE AND BEYOND

In its early days, Jamestown, Virginia, was almost entirely a community of men. Without wives and children the colonists saw little need to build substantial homes. Their first shelters were tents and rough wooden huts within a log stockade. The stockade had eight-foot walls of thick logs set vertically into the ground. According to George Percy the stockade was "triangle wise, having three bulwarks at every corner like a half moon, and four or five pieces of artillery mounted in them. We had made ourselves sufficiently strong for these savages."

Family and community were key to the success of the settlement. The founding fathers of Jamestown were bachelors until the Virginia Company sent a group of women to join them in the New World.

*A painting of Mount Vernon, George Washington's home, around
1792. Like other Southern plantations, Mount Vernon had grown
to match the family's expanding fortunes. During the 1760s and 1770s,
Washington enlarged the main house, added wings, constructed
several of the outbuildings, and increased the size of gardens.*

The stockade was a defense against attack by Native Americans, but it
was not a comfortable place to live. As time passed, some of the colonists
built log houses outside the fort. In 1620 a shipload of women reached
Virginia. The women quickly found husbands and set up housekeeping.
As families grew, so did the homes the colonists built.

By the middle of the 1600s many Virginia farmers owned prosperous
tobacco plantations. The planter's family lived in the "manor" or "great
house." At first the great house was not especially large. It usually
consisted of six rooms, three on the first floor and three upstairs. A brick
chimney stood at either end of the building. The family relaxed and ate
meals in the main room or "great hall."

Furniture in the early great houses was fairly simple. The family ate at a long plank table that rested on wooden trestles. These trestles somewhat resembled modern sawhorses. People sat at the table on stools or wooden benches called forms. Sometimes the bare floors were covered with animal hides or with straw mats bought from neighboring Indians.

Winters were fairly mild in the southern colonies, but summers could be brutally hot. A roaring fire for cooking would make the house unbearable, so the colonial kitchen was set up in an outbuilding across the yard from the great house. When the food was prepared servants

The slave Josiah Henson once wrote of his living conditions, "We lodged in log huts.... Wooden floors were an unknown luxury. In a single room were huddled, like cattle, ten or a dozen persons.... There were neither bedsteads nor furniture.... Our beds were collections of straw and old rags.... The wind whistled and the rain and snow blew in through the cracks, and the damp earth soaked in the moisture till the floor was miry as a pig-sty."

carried it to the manor in covered dishes.

As the years passed, plantation houses grew larger and more elaborate. Planters imported elegant furniture from Europe. Rooms were painted or papered in contrasting colors. A large house might boast a yellow room, a red room, a blue room, and so on. Mantels and banisters were carved with leaves, flowers, and curlicues.

The eighteenth-century plantation was like a village. The kitchen was only one of the buildings that clustered around the great house. There were workshops for carpenters, blacksmiths, and shoemakers. There were stables, tobacco barns, toolsheds, smokehouses, henhouses, and pigeon coops. In addition, the plantation had cabins for the many servants who kept the farm and household running smoothly.

Hired white servants and black slaves were housed in separate quarters. The white servants lived in tiny cabins of logs or unpainted boards. Their rough wooden furniture was made on the plantation. Slave quarters were even shabbier and more poorly furnished. Cabins for the slaves usually had dirt floors. The walls were riddled with cracks that let in winter air. The cold was especially uncomfortable for the slaves, who were used to very hot climates. They could not endure Virginia's sleet and wind. Many slaves lost toes and fingers to frostbite.

With all its slaves and servants, a plantation household could number more than one hundred people. Preparing food for so many was a massive undertaking that went on every day, 365 days a year.

LIVING TO EAT, EATING TO LIVE

It is hard to imagine how much food was devoured on an eighteenth-century plantation. One Virginia woman claimed that her household went through 2,700 pounds of pork, 20 beef cattle, 550 bushels of wheat, 4 hogsheads of rum, and 150 gallons of brandy in a single year. Her cooks used 100 pounds of flour each week. Most of this food and drink was consumed by her family and guests. Servants and slaves seldom tasted beef or even wheat bread. They lived chiefly on salt pork, corn bread, and

With just an open fire to work with, cooking was a challenge.
Iron pots filled with stew were hung from hooks or chimney bars just
above the flames. Other pots had short legs and sat on top of the coals.

hominy, a mush made from pounded corn kernels. Corn was a staple among the Indians, but it was not grown in Europe. The wealthier colonists preferred European foods. They looked down on corn as fit mainly for servants and animals.

In the great house the family sat down to a sumptuous dinner every midday. Josiah Quincy, a New Englander, visited Charleston, South Carolina, in 1773. He reported that his host served a three-course dinner followed by almonds, raisins, three kinds of olives, apples, oranges, and several expensive wines. The mistress of the house depended on servants to do the cooking and serving. But she planned the meals herself and oversaw their preparation.

The colonial homemaker sometimes turned for aid to one of the popular "cookery books." These books urged her to set an attractive table. The serving dishes should be arranged in a pattern with the highlight of the meal, the "grand conceit," at the center. A book called *The Complete Country Housewife* suggested placing gravy, soup, chicken, and bacon at one end of the table. At the other end would be a roast beef, surrounded by horseradish and pickles. Vegetable dishes and boiled pudding were to be arranged on either side. The grand conceit at the center was a giblet pie. And this was merely the first course. When all had eaten their fill

Dinner in the great house was served at midday, and the meal was often a lavish feast, lasting several hours.

servants cleared away the dishes and arranged the table once again. This time the grand conceit was a rich custard called tansy garnished with orange slices. On each side of the table were roasted hares and woodcocks on toast. Roast turkey and apple pie stood at each end. It is hard to believe that anyone could do more than gaze at the food in wonder.

By presenting a rich array of foods at dinner, the colonists showed off their wealth and power. Fashion was another form of visible display. When

A TASTY TREAT

The Indians introduced the colonists to many new food plants. Among them was the sweet potato, which became a popular ingredient in colonial cooking. Try this recipe for:

SWEET POTATO CORN BREAD

1 sweet potato	1/2 teaspoon baking soda
1 stick butter, softened	1 teaspoon cinnamon
4 eggs	1 small container plain yogurt
1/2 cup brown sugar	2 cups cornmeal

Prick the sweet potato in several places with a fork. Bake it at 350 degrees Fahrenheit for about 45 minutes. When it has cooled, peel off the skin. Mash the potato into pulp with a potato masher or wooden spoon. Add butter and mix thoroughly. Beat the eggs well in a small bowl. Add the sugar, baking soda, and cinnamon. Combine this with the potato mixture. Add the yogurt and cornmeal, stirring until smooth. Pour into a greased 9-by-9-inch baking pan and bake at 350 degrees Fahrenheit for 50 minutes. The bread should be golden brown and delicious.

they could afford to do so, the colonists were dedicated to following European styles.

SILKS AND SATINS

George Washington belonged to one of Virginia's most prominent famlies. In 1759 Washington ordered new clothes for his step-daughter, Patsy Custis. The order he sent to England included "six pair fine thread stockings, four pair worsted stockings, two caps, two pairs of ruffles, two tuckers, two fans, two masks, two bonnets, six pocket handkerchiefs, one cloth cloak, one coat of fashionable silk, six yards ribbon, two necklaces, [and] one pair silver sleeve buttons with stones." At the time Patsy Custis was only four years old.

Wealthy adults and children had elaborate wardrobes. Ladies of the eighteenth century wore tight-waisted dresses of satin, linen, or damask. Over the dress they wore an embroidered silk petticoat. Whalebone hoops made the petticoat spread wide. In 1710 petticoats measured six feet across. It must have been hard for the wearer to walk through a doorway or sit on a chair.

The colonial lady dreaded the sun. When she went outdoors she wore a velvet mask to protect her face. She made sure her complexion remained fashionably pale year-round.

Men, too, wore fancy clothing. A gentleman's jacket, or doublet, had

"Fashion Before Ease" — this cartoon is poking fun at the ladies who went to extremes for a small waistline.

slashes along the sleeves to reveal the fine linen shirt beneath. His cuffs and collar were trimmed with lace. A curling feather decorated his hat. A gentleman in full dress wore a light sword or rapier.

Ordinary people such as shopkeepers and small farmers dressed far more simply. Yet they imitated the gentry whenever they could. In Jamestown a gentleman complained that "our cowkeeper here on Sundays goes accoutered all in fresh flaming silk." To keep the "common folk" in their place, the gentry passed laws governing dress. A 1621 ordinance in Virginia forbade any but the owners of large plantations to wear gold embroidery.

Slaves wore simple, rough garments. Most of their clothing was made from the flax they harvested in the fields.

FRIENDS OF THE KING

Colonists from Virginia founded a settlement in present-day North Carolina in 1651. In 1663 King Charles II of England gave the land that is now North and South Carolina to eight of his friends at court. These landowners, or proprietors, controlled the growing colony. In 1712 the region divided into two separate colonies, North Carolina and South Carolina.

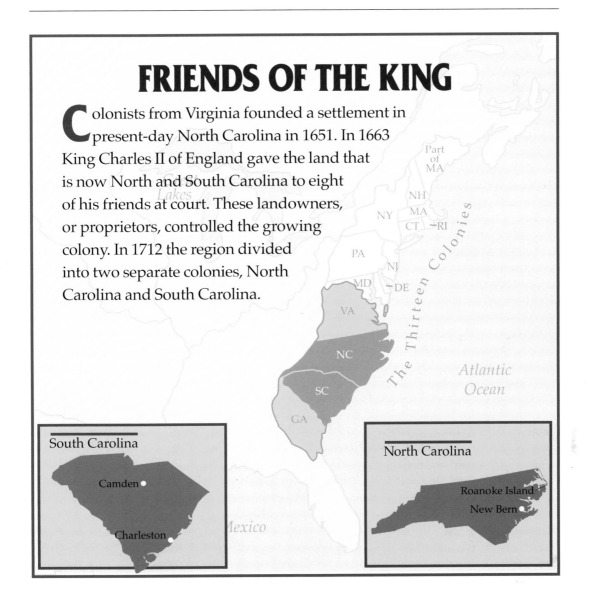

Servants and slaves had no chance to wear such finery. Their clothes were made of rough homespun cloth called tow. Clothing for slaves was cheap and practical. It was usually made on the plantation by a hired seamstress or by the slaves themselves. Slave children wore hand-me-downs until the clothes became ragged and fell to pieces.

Wealthy children like Patsy Custis were almost smothered by luxury. But slave children and the sons and daughters of the poor hardly knew what childhood was.

3
The Days of Childhood

"The children soon go [to work], the one here, the other there, and are treated like slaves and are brought up in ignorance like savages."

—A Swiss visitor to North Carolina in the early 1700s

NEVER TOO YOUNG

Families in the southern colonies tended to be large. Most women bore ten or twelve children in the course of a lifetime, and some even more. A Virginia woman named Nellie Custis Lewis wrote to a friend, "My dear mother has just recovered from her confinement with her twentieth child. It is a very fine girl, large and healthy. Mama has suffered extremely and is still weak."

To most colonial families, children were a great asset. On farms and plantations there was endless work to be done. Children helped their parents feed chickens, weed gardens, and herd sheep and cows. Little girls of six or seven learned to operate a spinning wheel. The spinning wheel was a machine for making linen thread. A twirling spindle twisted together the fibers of flax, a tall, graceful plant.

Some families were too poor to feed and clothe their many children. Parents often sent their sons and daughters to work for

Girls could be "bound out" by their parents as household servants, or apprenticed to become housekeepers, cooks, or needleworkers.

The skills of the cobbler were especially valued in colonial America, where shoes easily sprouted holes. Some cobblers traveled from house to house to make repairs.

others as servants or farmhands. The colonists encouraged children to enter the labor force. Promoters of the Georgia colony advertised that jobs were plentiful for women and children. A child who was "bound out" received meager food and lodging. The pay was pitifully low, but every extra penny was a help when times were hard.

Parents who were slaves had no choice about putting their children to work. Their offspring were the property of the master and mistress. From the time they were three or four, slave children began to work at simple chores. Sometimes a slave child was assigned to be the personal servant to one of the master's children. In these relationships, the two children grew very close. They ate together, played together, and sometimes shared a room at night. Yet the master's child could give orders, and the slave child had to obey. As they grew older, the gulf between them became wider and wider.

In 1620 the Virginia legislature arranged for one hundred English orphans to be sent to the colony. The legislature promised that the children would be: "educated and brought up in some good crafts, trades, or husbandry, whereby they may be enabled to get their living and maintain themselves when they shall…be out of their apprenticeships; and during their apprenticeships [they] shall have all things provided for them as shall be fit and requisite, as meat, drink, apparel, and other necessaries."

Under the apprentice system the hundred orphans and countless other children were bound to a master or mistress for seven years. During that time the apprentice worked for the master and lived in his or her household. The master had an obligation to teach the apprentice a useful trade. Boys learned to be joiners (cabinetmakers), coopers (barrelmakers), barbers, or blacksmiths. Girls usually apprenticed to dressmakers or milliners (makers of hats). The life of an apprentice was not an easy one. Yet apprenticeship offered children from poor families the chance to rise in society. Among the poor of the southern colonies it was the only means for getting an education.

READING, WRITING, AND BREAK TIME

"I thank God there are no free schools nor printing," wrote Governor Berkeley of Virginia in 1671. "I hope we shall not have [them] these hundred years." Berkeley feared that learning led to disobedience. He thought education might encourage people to rebel against the church and the government. Not many colonists held such extreme views. But tax-supported public schools were never established in the southern colonies. Children from poor families were not expected to learn to read or write. Education for the slaves was frowned upon. It was actually illegal in some communities.

Most well-to-do planters wanted their children to be educated properly. They hired tutors to teach their sons and daughters at home. Classes met in an outbuilding away from the great house. Cousins and neighbors could also attend these informal schools.

SCHOOL DAYS FOR A PRESIDENT

When he was eleven years old George Washington attended an old-field school near his family's plantation. The following year it closed, and he rode on horseback ten miles a day to attend another one. The year after that he took a ferry-boat across a small river to study in the town of Fredericksburg, Virginia. That was his last year of school attendance. George Washington's formal education ended when he was thirteen.

Philip Fithian tutored on a Virginia plantation called Nomini. He taught the planter's seven children and one of his nephews. Fithian left a detailed account of his teaching days:

"In the morning so soon as it is light a boy knocks on my door to make a fire. By the time I am dressed the children commonly enter the schoolroom, which is under the room I sleep in. I hear them say one lesson when the bell rings for 8 o'clock. The children then go out, and at half after 8 the bell rings for breakfast. After breakfast, which is generally about half after 9, we go into school and sit till 12, when the bell rings and they go out for noon. After dinner is over (which when we have no company is about half after 3) we go into school and sit till the bell rings at 5, when they separate till the next morning."

The day Fithian describes is slow and leisurely, broken by long interruptions for meals. The arrival of visitors would bring school to a complete halt. Classes might not resume for several days.

When they learned all that the tutor could teach them, planters' sons sometimes continued their education in Europe. They studied Latin, Greek, and history—the subjects a gentleman was expected to master.

Here at Jamestown, a boy is playing quoits, as he would have done in the 1600s. Today we call it ring toss, but the game is still the same.

Girls were seldom sent to study abroad, but a few attended "dame schools." A dame school was a school run by women. In some dame schools, girls and boys studied together as day students. In others, like those in Williamsburg, Virginia and Charleston, South Carolina, schoolmistresses ran boarding schools for girls only. The pupils learned French, needlework, drawing, and other ladylike accomplishments.

At times several neighboring families would donate funds to open a small private school for their children. Classes met in a hastily erected building in an unused field. Such fields had usually been planted in past years until the land was worn out. For this reason the schools were known as "old-field schools."

Overall, children in the southern colonies worked much more than they studied. But they managed to find time for playing, too.

ALL THE WORLD'S A PLAYGROUND

The children of the southern colonies would have been amazed at the array of toys on store shelves today. Even wealthy colonial children had only a few store-bought toys. There were dolls with lacy dresses and real hair adorned with beads and ribbons. There were little tin swords, whistles, and soldiers. Generally these toys came from England or France and were almost too costly to play with.

For the most part colonial children made their own toys. A chunk of wood could be whittled into a boat and floated downstream. A handful of dried cornhusks could be twisted to form a doll. But better than toys were the endless pleasures of the outdoors. Children built forts with fallen branches and pelted each other with hickory nuts. They climbed trees, ran races, and searched for birds' nests. The world was all a vast playground.

Groups of children played many traditional games such as tag, marbles, and hopscotch. Some of the games popular with younger children involved chanted rhymes. In one, a child became the "honey pot" by curling into a ball. Two others lifted the "pot" on their extended arms. They carried the curled-up child, chanting, "Carry your honey pot safe and sound / Or it will fall upon the ground." At any moment they would spread their arms and let the honey pot tumble into the grass.

On Sundays children did not have to work or attend school. But games were discouraged on the Sabbath. Sunday was a day of rest and prayer.

THE TOWN ON THE HARBOR

Charleston, South Carolina, was founded in 1670 on a spit of land between the Ashley and Cooper Rivers. The location was excellent because it offered a deep harbor. Charleston was the only major port in the southern colonies.

4
The Life of the Spirit

*"We did hang an awning, which is an old sail,
to three or four trees to shadow us from the sun....
Our seats [were] unhewed trees till we cut planks;
our pulpit a bar of wood nailed to two neighboring trees....
This was our church till we built a homely thing like
a barn, set upon cratchets [posts with a forked top],
covered with rafters, sedge, and earth."*

—CAPTAIN JOHN SMITH, DESCRIBING THE FIRST
CHURCH IN JAMESTOWN, VIRGINIA, 1608

THE ENGLISH CHURCH

Most of the colonists in the South were Protestants who belonged to the Anglican Church. The Anglican Church was known as the Church of England because the king had ordered that it should be followed by all his subjects. Today's Episcopal Church is the descendant of the Church of England that the colonists knew.

For many families, religion was not reserved just for the Sabbath.
Bible study and recitation were often daily events.

Jamestown's leaders made sure that everyone attended church regularly. On Sunday mornings a watchman went from door to door, checking to see that everyone was ready to go. At one time a Virginia law made nonattendance at church punishable by death. As far as historians know, however, no one was ever executed for sleeping in on Sundays.

During the 1600s most of the colonists took church attendance very seriously. According to Captain John Smith, "We had daily common prayer morning and evening; every Sunday two sermons; and every three months a holy communion till our minister died: but our prayers daily with an homily on Sundays we continued two or three years after, till more preachers came."

Church attendance dwindled in the 1700s, though the church buildings were much bigger and more comfortable. The pews were even cushioned. Well-to-do planters paid for the privilege of sitting in a special family pew. This pew was usually entered through a swinging door marked with the family name and coat of arms. Religion was not only a matter of learning and following the Bible. It was a means of enforcing the social order, in which some had immense wealth and others had little or nothing.

OTHER VOICES, OTHER FAITHS

In 1630 a large band of Puritans from England founded Boston in the Massachusetts Bay Colony. The Puritans were Protestants who believed in a strict interpretation of the Bible. By the late 1600s many Massachusetts Puritans feared that the people in their church were no longer carefully following its rules. They left Massachusetts and founded new settlements in the South.

Puritan communities grew up in Virginia and the Carolinas. Although they were few in numbers, the Puritans prospered. They worked hard as both farmers and merchants.

Another group of Protestants, from France, reached the southern colonies around 1685. These were the Huguenots. They were fleeing religious persecution in France, which was a strongly Roman Catholic

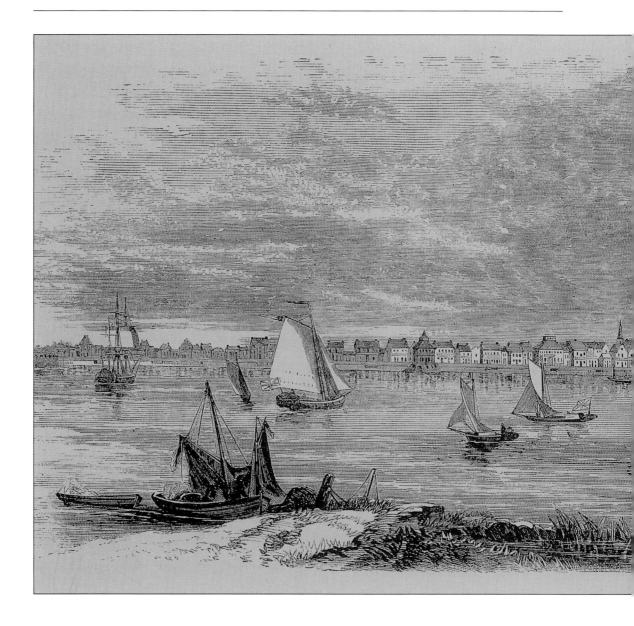

nation. In the 1570s thousands of Huguenots had been imprisoned and killed for their beliefs. When they heard rumors of renewed persecution in the 1680s, many Huguenots escaped to the New World. Refugees found peace and security in North and South Carolina. The New World gave them the religious freedom they had sought for more than a century.

The Huguenots formed close-knit farming communities. They were united by their faith and their memories of persecution in France. "They

Charleston was a city open to new ideas. In the 1700s its citizens could attend the first opera performed in the colonies, visit America's first museum, or worship in the nation's only Huguenot church.

live like one family," a visitor wrote, "each one rejoicing at the progress and elevation of his brethren."

The port of Charleston, South Carolina, was the most sophisticated town in the southern colonies. Merchant ships came to Charleston from all over the world. As a result Charleston learned to accept different religious faiths. Roman Catholics were looked down upon by many Protestant colonists, but they found respect and religious freedom in Charleston. Jewish synagogues also flourished in the city. Jews had long been persecuted in Europe. In the colonies they were often forbidden to worship openly. But in Charleston they had freedom they had seldom known before.

FROM AFRICAN SHORES

By 1740 about 150,000 people from Africa had been brought to the southern colonies as slaves. Africa is a vast continent, and the slaves came from diverse regions and cultures. Some were Muslims, followers of the ancient Islamic tradition. The rest practiced a variety of tribal religions. These religions were based on the idea that many gods and spirits controlled the universe. Each tribal religion had its own rules and rituals.

To the European colonists the chants and dances of African rituals seemed strange and even frightening. The colonists feared that the slaves were plotting rebellion when they gathered for a religious celebration. Slaves were forbidden to follow their old religious practices. Gradually the African religions seemed to disappear. But many slaves secretly kept their African traditions. Through rituals or spells, they called on the spirits for aid. Spells for healing, for winning a lover, and for cursing an enemy passed from one generation to the next.

Most slaveholders felt it was their duty to convert the Africans to Christianity. They tried to justify keeping the Africans in bondage with the claim that they were saving their souls. On Sundays the mistress or master of the house would hold church service for the slaves in a plantation outbuilding. They emphasized Bible verses that told servants to be loyal and obedient. They usually shied away from the passages that said all people were equal in the sight of God.

The slaves endured unimaginable hardships in the colonies. Christianity promised that a glorious reward awaited them in the next world. Religion offered them great comfort. But it was also used to stop them from fighting back.

In the hands of the slaveholders, religion was a tool for keeping people under control. It was one of the many methods the colonists used to maintain order and keep society running smoothly.

SLAVE OR CHRISTIAN?

Some colonists worried that it was morally wrong to hold fellow Christians as slaves. They argued that slaves who converted to Christianity should be granted their freedom. In 1667 the Virginia Assembly tried to settle the matter. The lawmakers declared that a slave who was baptized must remain a slave. Slaveholders could now baptize their slaves without fear of losing their property.

NEW HOPE FOR THE POOR

In eighteenth-century England thousands of people went to prison for failing to pay their debts. An English businessman named James Oglethorpe decided that debtors should be allowed to begin a new life in the colonies instead of being imprisoned. In 1733 Oglethorpe led a band of about 120 colonists to the site of present-day Savannah on the coast of Georgia. After a few years the plan to make Georgia a debtors' colony was abandoned. Like the other southern colonies Georgia had both large plantations and poor backcountry farms.

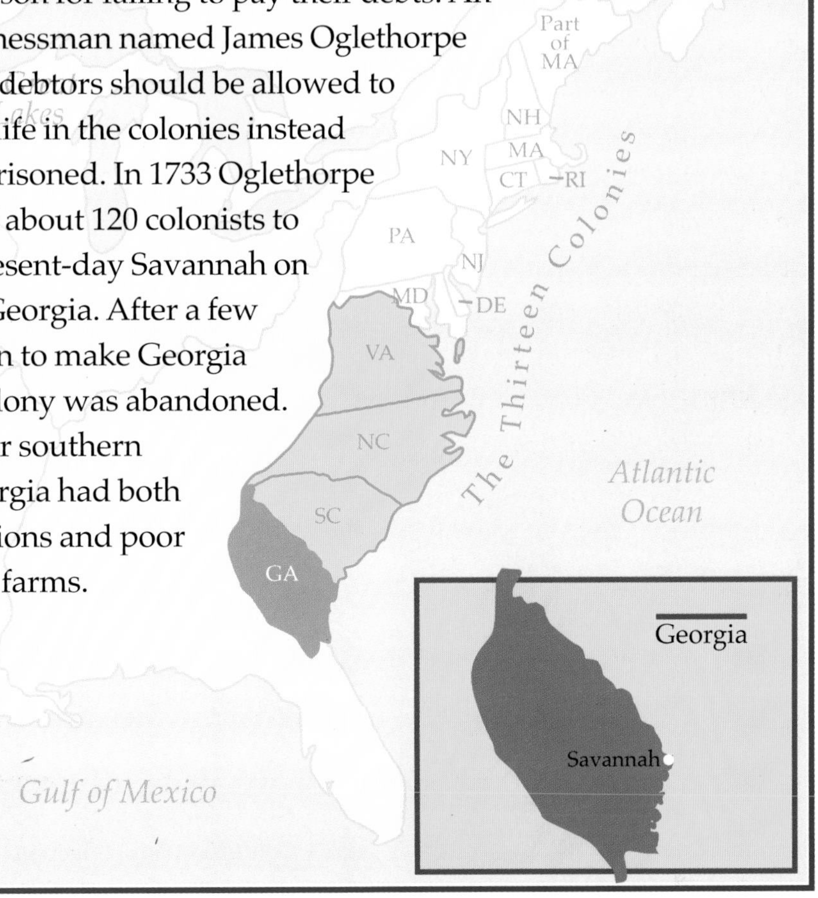

Part of MA

NH

NY   MA
      CT RI

PA

NJ

MD   DE

VA

The Thirteen Colonies

NC

Atlantic Ocean

SC

GA

Lakes

Gulf of Mexico

Georgia

Savannah

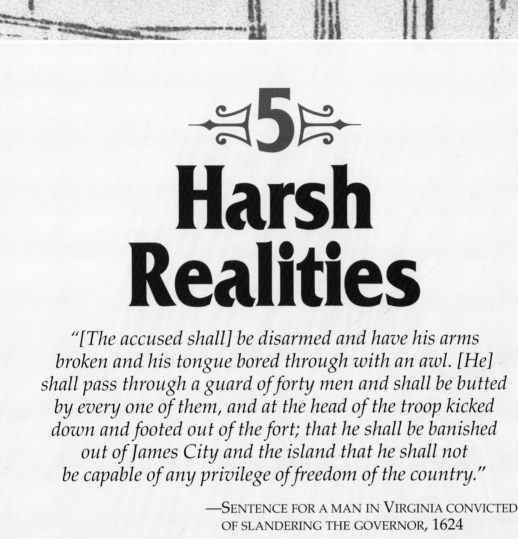

5
Harsh Realities

"[The accused shall] be disarmed and have his arms broken and his tongue bored through with an awl. [He] shall pass through a guard of forty men and shall be butted by every one of them, and at the head of the troop kicked down and footed out of the fort; that he shall be banished out of James City and the island that he shall not be capable of any privilege of freedom of the country."

—Sentence for a man in Virginia convicted of slandering the governor, 1624

THE WAGES OF SIN

By today's standards, the Jamestown man who slandered, or spread false rumors about, the governor met with a cruel and inhumane punishment. Such treatment was not unique to the southern colonies. The colonists were only continuing practices common back in England. In the New World, however, slander was an especially serious crime. The colonists needed all the help and support they could get from one another. If people spoke against their neighbors, the community could break down. A wise colonist learned to hold his or her tongue.

Colonial lawbreakers were rarely sent to prison. Instead judges used public humiliation as a punishment. A wrongdoer might be condemned to spend several days in the "bolts" or stocks. The stocks was a wooden device with openings for the prisoner's arms and legs. The pillory was a similar device, only the offender stood on his legs. Usually the pillory or stocks stood in front of the church or on the town square. There, the towns-people were free to stare, jeer, or even throw rotten fruits and vegetables.

A widely used punishment in the southern colonies was the ducking stool. It was often the fate of women regarded as "scolds." In 1634 a Virginia man named John Hartley witnessed a ducking and described it in a letter:

"The day afore yesterday at two of ye clock in the afternoon I saw this punishment given to one Betsey wife of John Tucker, who by ye violence of her tongue had made his house and ye neighborhood uncomfortable.… They had a machine for ye purpose.… It is a platform with small rollers or wheels and two upright posts between which works a lever by a rope fastened to its shorter or heavier end. At the end of ye longer arm is fixed a stool upon which Betsey was fastened by cords, her gown tied fast around her feet. The machine was then moved up to ye edge of ye pond, ye rope was slackened by ye officer and ye woman was allowed to go down under ye water for ye space of half a minute. Betsey had a stout stomach, and would not yield until she had allowed herself to be ducked several times.

The ducking stool was reserved for "witches and nagging women.' The practice was brought from England by the Puritans and quickly spread to the South.

At length she cried piteously "Let me go! Let me go, by God's help I will sin no more." Then they drew back ye machine, untied ye ropes and let her walk home in her wetted clothes a hopefully penitent woman."

During the early struggles of the Virginia colony Captain John Smith punished those who refused to work. He is said to have proclaimed that "he who does not work does not eat." If one of the colonists grumbled about laboring in the fields Smith made a public example of him. The complainer was forced to stand with his arms upraised. While the others watched and laughed, icy water was poured down the sleeves of the complainer's coat.

THE WORK OF MANY HANDS

"Workmen are dear [expensive] and scarce," wrote the Reverend John Urmstone, a North Carolina colonist, in 1711. "Had I servants and money, I might live very comfortably…[and] raise good corn of all sorts, and cattle, without any great labor or charges…but for want thereof [I] shall not make any advantage of my land…. I am forced to work hard with axe, hoe, and spade. I have not a stick to burn for any use but what I cut down with my own hands. I am forced to dig a garden, raise beans, peas, etc., with the assistance of a sorry wench my wife brought with her from England."

Like John Urmstone, many colonists owned large tracts of land that they could not farm without help. Some of these farmers contracted with indentured servants from England. In such an arrangement the planter paid for a person's passage to the New World. The man or woman worked off this debt by serving the planter for a given number of years. Seven years was the usual period of bondage, as it was in the apprentice system. But the master had no obligation to teach the indentured servant a trade.

In 1619 a Dutch merchant ship brought twenty Africans to Jamestown. They were the first slaves imported to the English colonies. At first, slaves were treated much like indentured servants. They were bound to their masters for seven years. The slaves were freed at the end of that time and

LIVES BUILT ON SMOKE

Europeans developed the habit of smoking tobacco in the early 1600s. Colonial planters could hardly meet the demand. Soon they began to depend heavily on slave labor. A good tobacco crop was extremely valuable. In fact, tobacco was so important in the southern colonies that it was often used as money. Some workers received their wages in bales of tobacco instead of silver and gold.

Tobacco was first grown at Jamestown in 1612.
The plants were sprouted in January, moved to a larger field
in May, and harvested in the August heat. Then the leaves had
to be cured, or hung in a barn for several months to dry.

CROATOAN

Many years before Jamestown was established, the English tried to start another colony in North America. In 1587 more than one hundred men, women, and children sailed from England to Roanoke Island off the coast of present-day North Carolina. When a supply ship arrived three years later the Roanoke colony had utterly vanished. The only trace was a mysterious word carved on the trunk of a tree: *Croatoan*. No one knows what it means. And no one has ever discovered what happened to these early settlers. Today Roanoke is often called the Lost Colony.

granted all the rights of white persons. After about forty years, however, new laws changed the status of slaves forever. From that time forward, slavery was a condition that lasted for life. In 1748 a Swedish botanist named Peter Kalm visited the colonies and wrote, "They [the slaves] have as good food as the rest of the servants, and they possess equal advantages in all things, except their being obliged to serve their whole lifetime, and get no other wages than what their master's goodness allows them."

As Kalm suggests, slaves had no rights, no assurance of decent treatment. Since they were property, their masters and mistresses could make use of them in any way they chose. If a master died or fell into debt, his slaves could be sold along with the livestock and furniture. Slave families were often separated, and children as young as seven were sold away from their parents.

Large crews of slave "field hands" worked in the tobacco fields. In South Carolina slaves planted and harvested rice. Indigo, a plant crop used in making blue dye, also depended on slave labor. Many planters in the southern colonies experimented with raising silkworms. Slave children gathered the silken cocoons and unwound the delicate threads with small, nimble fingers.

People who grew up surrounded by slaves became very dependent upon them. They could not imagine life without a staff of servants. When she retired to a country cottage, a Charleston widow named Eliza Pinckney wrote: "I shall keep young Eva to the drudgery part, to fetch wood and water and scour and learn as much as she is capable of cooking and washing. Maryann cooks, makes my bed, and makes my punch. Daphne works and makes the bread. Old Eva boils the cow's victuals, raises and fattens the poultry. Moses is employed from breakfast until 12 o'clock without-doors, after that in the house. Peg washes and milks." Eliza Pinckney had six slaves to manage her simple household.

Some slaves received training in skilled trades such as carpentry, leather tanning, or weaving. On some plantations they were allowed to earn and save money by practicing these trades. After careful saving, a slave could buy his or her freedom. Free African Americans worked for wages or ran businesses in the colonies.

WORKING FOR THE COMMON GOOD

Cooperation was vital if the settlers at early Jamestown were to survive. They had to work together for the good of all. Bakers made bread that was distributed free of charge. At first, all of the colonists were expected to work in the fields, and the harvest was divided among them. But leaders soon found that people worked harder when they tilled their own plots of land. Within a few years the colonists were running their own farms. In many other aspects of life, however, the colonists had to share responsibility and follow common rules.

Early laws in Virginia forbade the colonists to "wash any unclean linen [or] throw out water or suds of foul clothes" within the stockade. They were not to "make clean any kettle, pot or pan or suchlike vessel within 20 foot of the old well or new pump." The colonists hoped to keep their water supply pure. But sadly these measures had little effect on the colonists' health. The southern colonies were plagued with epidemics of smallpox, malaria, and other diseases. Malaria, or ague, is an illness that causes severe chills and fever. The colonists believed it was brought on by miasmas, or mists, that floated up from marshy ground. (The word malaria means "bad air.") They did not know that it was carried by the mosquitoes that swarmed from the marshes by the thousands.

Colonial women doctored their families, servants, and neighbors.

Colonial physicians believed that many illnesses were caused by the buildup of bad "humors" in the bloodstream. The only path to health, they thought, was to open a vein and drain the tainted blood.

They experimented with herbal brews, often laced with alcohol. A Virginia woman named Mary Johnson convinced the colonial assembly that she had developed a cure for cancer. The assembly awarded her a generous sum to dispense her medicine throughout the colony. To this day no one knows what Mary Johnson's treatment was or whether it really helped anyone.

Most people in the southern colonies lived on isolated farms. The few existing roads were overgrown with bushes and full of holes. A journey of forty miles could take several days. Here and there taverns offered food and lodging. But few travelers ever paid for a place to stay. Strangers were welcome at nearly any plantation along the road.

6 Making Merry

"The inhabitants are very courteous to travellers, who need no other recommendation than being human creatures. A stranger has no more to do but to inquire up the road where any gentleman or good housekeeper lives, and then he may depend upon being received with hospitality. This good-nature is so general among their people, that the gentry, when they go abroad, order their principal servants to entertain all visitors with everything the plantation affords."

—A TRAVELER IN VIRGINIA IN THE EARLY 1700s

SOUTHERN HOSPITALITY

On the southern plantation, life revolved around paying and receiving visits. Families rivaled one another to provide the finest meals and the most delightful company. By paying and receiving visits the colonists stayed in contact and kept abreast of the latest news. Visitors cut through the isolation of colonial life.

Some plantation owners posted a servant at the gate to keep watch on the road. It was the servant's duty to greet any passing stranger and urge him or her to come in. A guest was welcome to spend the night or even to stay for several days. Visitors were provided with the best food

Visiting friends or relatives could mean a journey of several days. Roads were rough and bumpy, so a visit might easily last a week.

Playing cards was a favorite pastime at dinner parties.

and beds the plantation could offer. One traveler claimed that "the poor planters who have but one bed will often sit up, or lie upon a form or couch all night, to make room for a weary traveller to repose himself after his journey."

After dinner the gentlemen usually smoked their pipes and talked about prices and politics. Perhaps someone brought out a deck of cards or a game of backgammon. The ladies retired to the drawing room for talk, cards, and music. Many young women studied singing. Others played the spinet or the harpsichord, keyboard instruments somewhat resembling today's piano.

Naturally not all visitors were strangers. Relatives and old friends frequently dropped in for a week or more. These visits were extended parties, full of feasting and laughter. For the children it was like an endless sleepover. In a letter a Virginia teenager wrote about her stay with family friends, cousins of George Washington: "I must tell you of our frolic after we went to our room. We took a large dish of bacon and beef; after that,

Fox hunting was a sport of the gentry. A large group of helpers improved the hunters' chances. Whippers-in scouted for the best hunting grounds, the huntsman directed the pack of hounds, and the earth stopper filled in the foxes' dens.

a bowl of Sago cream; and after that an apple pie. While we were eating the apple pie in bed—God bless you, making a great noise—in came Mr. [Corbin] Washington…and then Cousin Molly.… They joined us in eating the apple pie and then went out. After this we took it into our heads to want to eat oysters. We got up, put on our wrappers and went down in the cellar to get them; do you think Mr. Washington did follow us and scare us just to death. We went up though, and eat our oysters. We slept in the old lady's room too, and she sat laughing fit to kill herself at us."

ENTERTAINMENT TONIGHT!

In October 1737 a notice in the *Virginia Gazette* announced, "We have advices from Hanover County that on St. Andrew's Day there are to be horse races and several other diversions for the entertainment of the gentlemen and ladies." The notice went on to list horse races, foot races, a wrestling match, a fiddling contest, and a banquet enlivened by music and toasting. There would even be a beauty pageant of sorts, with a pair of silk stockings awarded to "the handsomest young country maid that appears in the field."

Horse racing was popular throughout the thirteen colonies, but it reached its height in Virginia. The Virginia quarterhorse was bred to run short distances at extraordinary speeds. Both men and women attended horse races. Horse racing, however, was a sport for the upper class. In one court case a Virginia tailor had to pay a heavy fine for entering a race reserved for gentlemen.

Hunting was strictly a sport for men and boys. They hunted deer, rabbits, squirrels, and wild ducks for both food and fun. Robert Beverley, a visitor to Virginia in the late 1600s, described hunting for "vermin"— opossums and raccoons:

"It is performed afoot with small dogs in the night by the light of the moon or stars. Wherever the dog barks, you may depend upon finding the game, and this alarm draws men and dogs that way. [When the prey has been treed] they detach a nimble fellow up after it, who must have a

WILD HORSES

In the early days of the colonies, fences were poor or nonexistent. Many of the colonists' horses escaped into the forests. Over the years these horses became completely wild. The colonists captured them for sport, sometimes using dogs to track them down. These wild horses were swift and beautiful, but they were difficult to tame. They seldom made good saddle horses.

scuffle with the beast before he can throw it down to the dogs, and then the sport increases to see the vermin encounter those little curs."

Beverley also described hare hunting. If the hare hid in a hollow log the hunters lighted a fire and drove it out with the smoke. "If they have a mind to spare their lives," Beverley explained, "upon turning them loose they will be as fit as ever to hunt at another time, for the mischief done them by the smoke immediately wears off."

Another male amusement was the bloody sport of cockfighting. A pair of roosters fought to the death with razor-sharp spurs fastened to their feet. Onlookers bet on the outcome. A northern visitor to Chesapeake Bay gives a vivid account: "The little heroes appeared trained to the business and not the least disconcerted by the crowd or shouting. They stepped about with great apparent pride and dignity.... Frequently one, or both, were struck dead at the first blow, but they often fought after being repeatedly pierced, as long as they were able to crawl." Such blood sports as cockfighting flourished in Europe. Like so much else, they came with the colonists to the New World.

Not all entertainment featured violence or speed. Men and women, young and old, all loved to dance. Dances ranged from formal balls to impromptu gatherings at someone's home. Poor country people danced lively jigs and reels. Well-to-do planters and their families learned the stately minuet and other dances popular in Europe.

Entertainment for the gentry was more work for the slaves. At races, slaves tended the horses and waited on the spectators. They handled the dogs on hunts, and dressed the meat when an animal was killed. At balls, slaves handed out food and drink. They scrubbed and polished to put everything in order when the guests departed. Yet the slaves managed to find enjoyment in life, despite its hardships. Sometimes, to relieve the drudgery, they sang as they worked in the rice and tobacco fields. In the evenings they told stories, many of them tracing back to African legends. Church service was a special time when the slaves could gather without having to work. At church there was music, good fellowship, and celebration.

A wedding in the slave quarters. Slaves were encouraged to marry and start a family. It provided them support and the sense of a normal life. But for the master, it meant children—the next generations of slaves.

THE HIGHER SPHERES

In 1665 a troupe of players put on a show called *Ye Bear and Ye Cub* in Accomac County, Virginia. Some of the local citizens were outraged. They believed that the theater bred laziness and immorality, distracting people from wiser pursuits. Finally the magistrate ordered the players to perform for him so he could decide whether the play was harmful. He liked it so much that he told them to put it on for the whole county.

The theater found greater favor in the South than anywhere else in the colonies. The first theater in America opened in Williamsburg, Virginia, in 1716. In Charleston, South Carolina, actors performed in the courthouse until a theater opened there in 1737. Traveling players went throughout the southern colonies, performing at county fairs and other public gatherings. Shakespearean plays were very popular. The colonists also enjoyed tragedies and comedies by other English playwrights. Most of these works have long since been forgotten. To this day no copy of *Ye Bear and Ye Cub* has ever been found.

The southern colonies did not produce many novelists or poets, but planters often had large private libraries. Most of their books came from England. Young girls read romantic novels in much the way they follow television soap operas today. Then as now a sad story was an excuse for a good cry. A Virginia teenager wrote to a friend, "I have spent the morning in reading Lady Julia Mandeville, and was much affected. Indeed I think I never cried more in my life reading a novel…. We must go down, but I am afraid both Sister's and my eyes will betray us."

Many colonial homes were decorated with paintings. During the 1700s artists began to advertise their services. Most of them boasted of a variety of talents. They offered to paint portraits and landscapes, as well as coats of arms on carriages, doors, and fireplaces. Many of these artists were also housepainters by trade.

Sometimes rich planters arranged to have family portraits done in Europe. The planter would send descriptions of himself, his wife, and his children to a well-known English painter. The painter created a "likeness" by following the descriptions—such as dark hair, high cheekbones, green eyes, and so on. It didn't matter if painter and subject ever met. Planters didn't really want their family portraits to be true to life. They wanted to be depicted as nobles without any flaws.

With the founding of Jamestown in 1607 England began a colonial empire in North America. In 1776 that empire lost an important possession. Delegates from the thirteen colonies signed the Declaration of Independence, severing ties with the mother country. The colonies won their freedom at the end of a long and bloody war. After more than 150 years, the colonial era was over. The former colonies joined to form a new nation, the United States of America.

LEADERS OF A NATION

Three of the most outstanding leaders of the new United States grew up in colonial Virginia. Thomas Jefferson was the chief author of the Declaration of Independence. James Madison did most of the writing of the U.S. Constitution. And George Washington became the nation's first president.

Glossary

accoutered: Decked out in finery.

asset: An item of value.

awl: Sharp metal instrument used for punching holes in leather.

backgammon: Board game in which the pieces are moved according to the throws of the dice.

bulwark: A solid wall-like structure built for defense.

coat of arms: Symbolic picture used to represent a particular family.

damask: Silk, cotton, or linen fabric with a woven pattern; the pattern is the color of the fabric itself.

disconcerted: Startled, made uncomfortable.

drudgery: Boring, repetitive work.

enmesh: To catch in a tangle or net.

flax: Tall, graceful plant whose dried fibers are used in making linen thread.

flux: Severe diarrhea.

frolic: Lively party.

gem: Precious stone.

gentry: The wealthy upper class.

hare: Animal in the rabbit family, larger than the common cottontail.

hogshead: Large barrel.

homily: Sermon or moralizing lecture.

hominy: Mush made from mashed corn kernels.

husbandry: The care of a household; the management of farming and domestic animals.

magistrate: Local judge.

manor: Large, elegant house surrounded by extensive grounds.

miasma: Damp, cool mist once thought to carry disease.

penitent: Sorry.

rapier: Small, light sword.

repose: Rest.

rival: To compete.

Sabbath: The seventh day of the week—observed as a day of rest and worship—Sunday for most Christians.

scold: One who speaks sharply and finds fault.

sedge: Thick, grasslike plant.

slander: To make a false statement that damages a person's reputation.

spindle: Slender wooden stick, part of a spinning wheel.

spit: Narrow sandy peninsula.

stockade: Fort surrounded by high log walls.

sumptuous: Very magnificent and rich.

trestle: Wooden support for a table, resembling a sawhorse.

tucker: Frill of lace worn around the neck or shoulders.

unhewed: Uncut, rough (usually referring to logs).

victuals: Food.

wench: Young girl of the lower classes, often a servant.

woodcock: Small game bird found in marshy areas.

worsted: Fabric made from twisted woolen yarn.

wrapper: Light robe or coat.

A NOTE ABOUT SPELLING

If you were to read a letter or diary written in colonial days, you would be amazed by the way some of the words are spelled. The word wind might be spelled wynd or wynde. Words would be capitalized almost at random. Until the middle of the 1700s, English-language spelling had few standard rules. People spelled words more or less as they wished. The results are certainly interesting, but they can be confusing, too. To clarify the meaning for the readers of this book, I have modernized the spelling in all quotes from colonial documents.

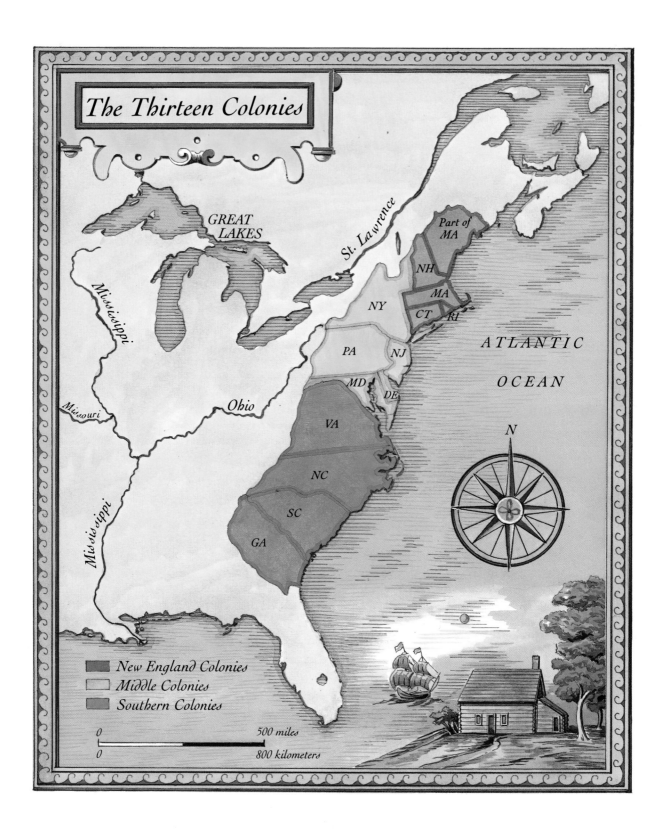

The Thirteen Colonies

GREAT LAKES

Mississippi

St. Lawrence

Missouri

Ohio

Mississippi

Mississippi

Part of MA

NH

NY

MA

CT

RI

PA

NJ

MD

DE

VA

NC

SC

GA

ATLANTIC

OCEAN

N

New England Colonies
Middle Colonies
Southern Colonies

0   500 miles

0   800 kilometers

The Southern Colonies in Time

1587—Sir Walter Raleigh sends a band of English settlers to Roanoke Island off the coast of North Carolina.

1590—A supply ship reaches Roanoke Island and discovers that the colony has vanished.

1607—English colonists found Jamestown on the James River in Virginia; it is the first permanent English settlement in North America.

1619—A Dutch trading ship brings the first African slaves to Virginia.

1633—Middle Plantation (now Williamsburg) is founded in Virginia.

1651—Colonists from Virginia settle in present-day North and South Carolina.

1663—King Charles II of England gives Carolina to eight of his friends at court, known as the Lords Proprietors.

1670—The port of Charleston is founded on the Ashley and Cooper Rivers in what is now South Carolina.

1699—Jamestown is destroyed by fire; Williamsburg becomes the capital of Virginia.

1712—Carolina divides into two separate colonies, North and South Carolina.

1716—The first theater in the colonies opens in Williamsburg.

1733—James Oglethorpe leads a group of English colonists to the site of Savannah in present-day Georgia.

1776—Virginian Thomas Jefferson writes the Declaration of Independence, severing ties between the colonies and Great Britain.

1781—Colonial troops defeat the British at the Battle of Yorktown in Virginia, the last major battle of the American Revolution.

1783—The Treaty of Paris ends the Revolutionary War; the former colonies form a new and independent nation.

Places to Visit

NORTH CAROLINA

Roanoke Island:
The ill-fated Roanoke settlement is remembered through pictures and relics at the Fort Raleigh Museum. During the summer visitors can enjoy an outdoor performance of the play *"The Lost Colony."*

Tryon House, New Bern:
In the eighteenth century this elegant house was home to the royal governor of North Carolina. To annoy the British, rebel leaders held a meeting here in 1774, shortly before the American Revolution began.

SOUTH CAROLINA

Charles Towne Landing, Charleston:
This reconstructed community provides a glimpse of life in Charleston's original settlement. Among the attractions is a fully rigged re-creation of a seventeenth-century trading vessel.

Historic Camden, Camden:
Camden's historic area features several buildings that date to the middle of the eighteenth century. Kershaw House was the headquarters of Lord Cornwallis, a leading British general during the American Revolution.

VIRGINIA

Berkeley Plantation, near Richmond:
Berkeley Plantation was the birthplace of William Henry Harrison, ninth president of the United States. The handsome manor house, built in 1726, has been restored to look as it did during the eighteenth century.

Historic Williamsburg, Williamsburg:
This restored colonial town draws more than a million visitors each year. Some eighty buildings have been fully reconstructed. Guides in period costumes demonstrate blacksmithing, barrel making, spinning, and other colonial trades. Williamsburg served as the capital of the Virginia colony from 1699 to 1776. Its restoration began in 1926 with money donated by multimillionaire John D. Rockefeller.

St. Luke's Church, Smithfield:
Built in 1632, this is the oldest surviving brick church in the United States.

To Learn More...

BOOKS

Fleming, Alice. *George Washington Wasn't Always Old.* Danbury, CT: Children's Press, 1991.

Fritz, Jean. *The Double Life of Pocahontas.* Tarrytown, NY: Marshall Cavendish, 1991.

Hakim, Joy. *Making Thirteen Colonies.* New York: Oxford University Press, 1993.

Hilton, Suzanne. *The World of Young Thomas Jefferson.* New York: Walker, 1986.

Hine, Darlene. *The Age of Discovery and the Slave Trade.* New York: Chelsea House, 1995.

Kent, Deborah. *African-Americans in the Thirteen Colonies.* Danbury, CT: Children's Press, 1996.

Perl, Lila. *Slumps, Grunts, and Snicker-doodles: What Colonial America Ate and Why.* New York: Clarion Books, 1979.

Reische, Diana. *Founding the American Colonies.* New York: Franklin Watts, 1989.

Smith, Carter, ed. *Daily Life: A Sourcebook on Colonial America.* Brookfield, CT: Millbrook, 1992.

Turkle, Brinton. *If You Lived in Colonial Times.* New York: Scholastic, 1992.

Warner, John F. *Colonial American Home Life.* New York: Franklin Watts, 1993.

Washburne, Carolyn Kott. *A Multicultural Portrait of Colonial Life.* New York: Marshall Cavendish, 1994.

AUDIO AND VIDEO

Colonial Williamsburg. One 30-minute videocassette. Explores life in the capital of colonial Virginia. Video Tours, Glastonbury, CT. 1993.

WEBSITES*

We're History: Welcome to Virginia, includes information about Virginia's Native Americans, and about life among blacks and whites in colonial Virginia. http://www.itshistory.com/vaindex.html

Websites change from time to time. For additional on-line information, check with your media specialist at your local library.

Bibliography

Earle, Alice Morse. *Colonial Dames and Good Wives*. New York: Frederick Ungar, 1962. (Originally published by Houghton Mifflin, Boston, 1895.)

———. *Home Life in Colonial Days*. Stockbridge, MA: Berkshire House, 1993. (Originally published by Macmillan, New York, 1898.)

Encyclopedia Britannica. *The Annals of America*. Vol. 1: 1493-1754, *Discovering a New World*. Chicago: Encyclopedia Britannica, 1976.

Hawke, David Freeman. *Everyday Life in Early America*. New York: Harper & Row, 1988.

Spruill, Julia Cherry. *Life and Work in the Southern Colonies*. Chapel Hill: University of North Carolina Press, 1938.

Starkey, Marion L. *Land Where Our Fathers Died: The Settling of the Eastern Shores, 1607-1735*. Garden City, NY: Doubleday, 1962.

Train, Arthur, Jr. *The Story of Everyday Things*. New York: Harper & Brothers, 1941.

Notes on Quotes

The quotations from this book are from the following sources:

The New Discovered Land
Page 7, "Our men were destroyed by cruel diseases": Starkey, *Land Where Our Fathers Died*, p. 19.

Home Sweet Home
Page 13, "We had no houses to cover us": Train, *The Story of Everyday Things*, 1941, p. 102.

Page 14, "triangle wise, having three bulwarks": *Land Where Our Fathers Died*, p. 15.

Page 20, "six pair fine thread stockings": Spruill, *Life and Work in the Southern Colonies*, p. 133.

Page 22, "our cowkeeper here on Sundays": *The Story of Everyday Things*, p. 112.

The Days of Childhood
Page 25, "The children soon go to work": *Life and Work in the Southern Colonies*, p. 57.

Page 26, "My dear mother has just recovered": *Life and Work in the Southern Colonies*, p. 47.

Page 28, "educated and brought up in some good crafts": Encyclopedia Britannica, *The Annals of America*, Vol. 1, p. 60.

Page 28, "I thank God there are no free schools": *The Story of Everyday Things*, p. 121.

Page 29, "In the morning so soon as it is light": *Life and Work in the Southern Colonies*, p. 186.

The Life of the Spirit
Page 33, "We did hang an awning": Earle, *Home Life in Colonial Days*, p. 381.

Page 35, "We had daily common prayer": *Home Life in Colonial Days*, pp. 381–382.

Page 36–37, "They live like one family": *Land Where Our Fathers Died*, p. 228.

Harsh Realities
Page 41, "The accused shall have his arms broken": Hawke, *Everyday Life in Early America*, p. 107.

Page 43, "The day afore yesterday": Earle, *Colonial Dames and Good Wives*, pp. 93–94.

Page 44, "Workmen are dear and scarce": *The Annals of America*, Vol. 1, p. 329.

Page 47, "I shall keep young Eva to the drudgery part": *Life and Work in the Southern Colonies*, p. 75.

Page 47, "Wash any unclean linen": *Life and Work in the Southern Colonies*, p. 6.

Making Merry
Page 51, "The inhabitants are very courteous": *Home Life in Colonial Days*, p. 360.

Page 53, "The poor planter who has but one bed": *Home Life in Colonial Days*, p. 360.

Page 54–55, "I must tell you of our frolic": *Colonial Dames and Good Wives*, pp. 198–199.

Page 55, "We have advices from Hanover County": *Colonial Dames and Good Wives,* pp. 207–208.

Page 55, "It is performed afoot with small dogs in the night": *Everyday Life in Early America,* p. 97.

Page 56, "If they have a mind to spare their lives": *Everyday Life in Early America,* pp. 96–97.

Page 56, "The little heroes appeared trained to the business": *Everyday Life in Early America,* p. 99.

Page 58, "I have spent the morning in reading Lady Julia Mandeville": *Colonial Dames and Good Wives,* p. 19.

Index

About the Author

Deborah Kent grew up in Little Falls, New Jersey, and received her Bachelor of Arts degree from Oberlin College in Ohio. She went on to earn a Master's Degree from Smith College School for Social Work and took a job at the University Settlement House in New York City. After four years in social work, she decided to pursue her lifelong interest in writing. She moved to San Miguel de Allende, Mexico, a charming town with a colony of foreign writers and artists. In San Miguel she wrote her first novel for young adults, *Belonging*.

Today Deborah has more than a dozen novels to her credit, and has written many nonfiction children's books as well. She lives in Chicago with her husband, children's book author R. Conrad Stein, and their daughter, Janna.

"When I was in school," Deborah recalls, "I thought history was boring. We learned about wars and political leaders, but seldom heard about ordinary people. Back then I could never have guessed that some day I would study history for fun, and that I would even write books about it! I am fascinated not by generals and presidents, but by the women, men, and children of the past whose names have been nearly forgotten. It is exciting to explore the world they knew and to try to imagine how they lived their lives."